CHECKERBOARD BIOGRAPHIES

AMANDA GORMAN

MEGAN BORGERT-SPANIOL

Checkerboard
Library

An Imprint of Abdo Publishing
abdobooks.com

ABDOBOOKS.COM

Published by Abdo Publishing, a division of ABDO, PO Box 398166, Minneapolis, Minnesota 55439.
Copyright © 2022 by Abdo Consulting Group, Inc. International copyrights reserved in all countries.
No part of this book may be reproduced in any form without written permission from the publisher.
Checkerboard Library™ is a trademark and logo of Abdo Publishing.

Printed in the United States of America, North Mankato, Minnesota
052021
092021

THIS BOOK CONTAINS
RECYCLED MATERIALS

Design and Production: Mighty Media, Inc.
Editor: Liz Salzmann
Cover Photograph: Stephen Smith/AP Images
Interior Photographs: Carlos M. Vazquez II/Flickr, pp. 5, 29; Carlos M. Vazquez II/Wikimedia Commons,
    p. 27; Dwight Carter/Penn State/Flickr, p. 7; Mark's Photo/iStockphoto, p. 29 (top); Patrick Semansky/
    AP Images, p. 21; Peter Stevens/Flickr, p. 9; Ryan Lash/Flickr, p. 13; Shawn Miller/Flickr, pp. 11, 28 (top);
    Shutterstock Images, pp. 9 (paper clip), 15, 17, 28; Sipa USA/AP Images, p. 23; Win McNamee/AP
    Images, p. 19; ZUMA Press/Alamy, p. 25

Library of Congress Control Number: 2021932878

Publisher's Cataloging-in-Publication Data

Names: Borgert-Spaniol, Megan, author.
Title: Amanda Gorman / by Megan Borgert-Spaniol
Description: Minneapolis, Minnesota : Abdo Publishing, 2022 | Series: Checkerboard biographies | Includes
    online resources and index.
Identifiers: ISBN 9781532195990 (lib. bdg.) | ISBN 9781098216856 (ebook)
Subjects: LCSH: Poets--Biography--Juvenile literature. | Poets laureate--Biography--Juvenile literature.
    | African American women poets--Biography--Juvenile literature. | Women activists--Biography--
    Juvenile literature. | Feminist poetry, English--Juvenile literature.
Classification: DDC 928.1--dc23

CONTENTS

CHAPTER 1

INAUGURAL POET

In January 2021, Amanda Gorman became the youngest poet to perform at a US presidential **inauguration**. In April 2017, she had become the first National Youth **Poet Laureate**. Before that, she was the first Youth Poet Laureate of Los Angeles, California.

Growing up, Gorman had a speech **impediment**. It made certain sounds difficult for her to pronounce. Because of her trouble speaking, Gorman expressed herself through writing. In time, she became a poet.

Gorman had only recently graduated from college when she spoke at the presidential inauguration. There, she delivered a moving poem about the nation overcoming challenges. Gorman's performance launched her into the national spotlight. The future was bright for this young poet.

> " I don't think I would have been able to write that inauguration poem if I hadn't lived every day of my life as if that was the place I was going to get. "

Gorman loves to express herself through fashion. She said, "Through my fashion, and the way I wear my hair, I can pay homage to my Black heritage, to my sociopolitical beliefs, and my personality."

CHAPTER 2

YOUNG WRITER

Amanda S.C. Gorman was born on March 7, 1998, in Los Angeles, California. She has a twin sister, Gabrielle, and an older brother, Spencer. Amanda was raised in Los Angeles by her mother, Joan Wicks. Wicks taught English at a middle school.

Amanda was born with an **auditory** processing **disorder**. This meant she could hear normally, but her brain took longer to make sense of the sounds. Gorman also had a speech **impediment**. She struggled to pronounce certain sounds, especially the letter *R*.

Because of her impediment, Amanda turned to writing to express herself. When she was in the third grade, she wrote her first poems. The poems expressed how she felt like an outsider among other kids her age. Amanda found a sense of power in writing about these feelings. Her teacher encouraged her to keep writing. Amanda worked hard on improving her poetry.

Young Amanda looked up to the African American poet Maya Angelou. She said Angelou made her want to be both a good poet and a good person.

CHAPTER 3

YOUTH POET LAUREATE

Amanda attended high school at New Roads School in Santa Monica, California. During this time, she began to share her writing talents. When she was 15, she started teaching creative writing at the school where her mom taught. This work helped Amanda realize the importance of **literacy**, especially in the lives of students of color.

In 2014, a group of local literary organizations launched the Los Angeles Youth **Poet Laureate** Program. Amanda applied to the program, and she was selected for the honor! At 16 years old, she was named the first Youth Poet Laureate of Los Angeles.

In 2015, she published a book of poems called *The One for Whom Food Is Not Enough*. Amanda also wanted to contribute to **empowering** youth through education. The next year, she founded One Pen One Page. This organization provided free creative writing programs for children and teenagers.

BIO BASICS

NAME: Amanda Gorman

BIRTH: March 7, 1998, Los Angeles, California

FAMOUS FOR: reciting her poem "The Hill We Climb" at the 2021 presidential inauguration

ACHIEVEMENTS: becoming the first Youth Poet Laureate of Los Angeles; becoming the first National Youth Poet Laureate; becoming the youngest inaugural poet in US history; being the first poet to perform at the Super Bowl

" I love Black poets. I love that as a Black girl, I get to participate in that legacy. "

CHAPTER 4

HARVARD

Gorman graduated from high school in 2016. From there, she moved across the country for college. She studied **sociology** at Harvard University in Cambridge, Massachusetts.

In addition to her studies, Gorman continued her work as a **poet laureate**. The same year she started college, she became a finalist for the first-ever National Youth Poet Laureate. And in 2017, Gorman was the one to receive the honor!

At 19 years old, Gorman was representing poetry, **literacy**, and education across the nation. She traveled the country performing her poetry. She also received a grant to pursue a project she called Generation **Empathy**. For this project, Gorman **documented** the lives of young leaders across the United States. Her goal was to present their stories as a **virtual reality** experience.

66 It's so exciting to help give youth the platform and access they need to be rising voices in the literary world. 99

In September 2017, Gorman performed her poem "In This Place (An American Lyric)" at the US Library of Congress in Washington, DC.

As Gorman performed her poetry across the country, she struggled with her speech **impediment**. She considered cutting words that were difficult for her to pronounce. She worried that listeners wouldn't understand what she was saying. But Gorman stayed true to herself and her work. She told herself that if people didn't understand her, they could read the poem later.

As Gorman performed more, she learned to pronounce the letters she had struggled with. She also recited the song "Aaron Burr, Sir" from the musical *Hamilton*. The song was full of words that included the letter *R*. She thought this would help her say *R* sounds. Gorman's work paid off. She slowly overcame her speech impediment.

"Now I really look at [my impediment] as a strength because ... when I was brave enough to try to take those words from the page onto the stage, I brought with me this understanding of the complexity of sound, pronunciation, emphasis."

Gorman spoke alongside other youth leaders at a New York TED-Ed event in November 2018.

CHAPTER 5

INAUGURATION INVITATION

Gorman graduated from Harvard in 2020. After college, she moved back to Los Angeles. But it wasn't long before she was preparing for a trip back to the East Coast.

In December 2020, Gorman had a video call with the presidential **inaugural** committee. This committee was organizing the upcoming inauguration of US president-elect Joe Biden. Biden's wife, Jill, had seen one of Gorman's performances at the US Library of Congress in Washington, DC. Jill suggested that Gorman read a poem at Biden's inauguration!

Gorman was thrilled at the invitation to speak at such a historic event. At the time, the United States was suffering. Hundreds of thousands of Americans had died over the past year due to the **COVID-19 pandemic**. The nation was also facing political **unrest** after Biden's election. Gorman wanted to write a poem that sparked a sense of hope and unity in Americans.

Gorman at the American Black Film Festival Honors in February 2020

To get inspired, Gorman read the speeches of American leaders, including Abraham Lincoln and Martin Luther King Jr. She studied how these speakers tried to bring people together during times of division. Gorman also listened to music from *Hamilton*.

The writing process was slow. Gorman completed just a few lines a day. Then on January 6, 2021, a riot broke out at the US Capitol. Crowds of people who were angry about Biden's election stormed inside the building. Many people were injured in the attack. Back in Los Angeles, Gorman knew she wanted to acknowledge the riot at the upcoming **inauguration**. That night, she stayed up late to finish her poem.

Gorman titled her work "The Hill We Climb." With the piece now written, she began to practice reciting it. Gorman did not want to stumble over her words at the inauguration. So, she read the poem aloud over and over again.

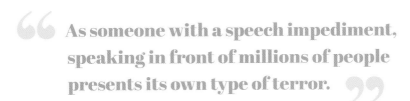

As someone with a speech impediment, speaking in front of millions of people presents its own type of terror.

Gorman referenced the January 6 Capitol riot in her poem. It includes the line, "We've seen a force that would shatter our nation rather than share it."

CHAPTER 6

"THE HILL WE CLIMB"

On January 20, Gorman watched as Biden was inaugurated. She listened to his first address as president. She watched Lady Gaga sing the national **anthem**. As Gorman enjoyed the ceremony, she also felt nervous about her upcoming reading. She worried she would trip on her way up to the **podium**. She worried her hands would be too cold to turn the pages as she read.

Then, it was time for Gorman to take the stage. Millions of Americans watched from their homes as Gorman stepped up to the podium and smiled. She first greeted the president, vice president, America, and the world. Then, she read her poem. "When the day comes we ask ourselves, where can we find light in this never-ending shade?" she began.

AMANDA'S MANTRA

To calm herself before every performance, Gorman recites a **mantra** to herself. She closes her eyes and says, "I'm the daughter of Black writers who are descended from Freedom Fighters who broke their chains and changed the world. They call me."

Gorman attended the inauguration with her mother (*left*).
Attendees wore masks to protect against COVID-19.

Gorman delivered her poem over the next five and a half minutes. She looked out over the crowd as she spoke clearly and forcefully. She had practiced reciting her poem many times. She rarely needed to look down to read it.

"The Hill We Climb" addressed the nation's imperfect past, present challenges, and hopeful future. It spoke of rising, rebuilding, and recovering. As Gorman spoke, she used hand motions to accompany her words. Gorman concluded her poem with the line, "For there is always light, if only we're brave enough to see it. If only we're brave enough to be it."

Most Americans had never heard of Amanda Gorman before the 2021 **inauguration**. But by the time Gorman stepped off the **podium**, she had become a national

CAGED BIRD RING

At the inauguration, Gorman wore a ring that Oprah Winfrey had given her. The ring had a small statue of a bird inside a cage. The ring honored the poet Maya Angelou and her book, *I Know Why the Caged Bird Sings.*

President Joe Biden (*front row left*) and Vice President Kamala Harris (*front row right*) watch as Gorman recites her poem.

sensation. At 22 years old, she was the youngest poet to perform at a US presidential **inauguration**. Viewers across the country were amazed by the bold presence and wise words of the young poet.

CHAPTER 7

LAUNCH TO FAME

When Gorman was writing "The Hill We Climb," she hadn't thought how it might change her life. She was only focused on writing something worthy of the historic moment. But after the **inauguration**, it didn't take long for Gorman to realize things had changed. Her first clue was her social media following. She couldn't open her Instagram app because of all her new followers. In just 24 hours, she gained more than 2 million of them!

Everyone wanted to know more about the 22-year-old poet. Over the following days, Gorman was interviewed by news reporters and talk show hosts. National leaders and celebrities were posting about her on social media.

Gorman also had two books coming out later that year. After the inauguration, the books moved to the top of Amazon's best seller list. People were buying Gorman's books before they had even come out!

HUGS ALL AROUND

After the inauguration ceremony, Gorman was thrilled to hug some of her idols. They included Lady Gaga and former First Lady Michelle Obama.

Gorman poses for a photo with Lady Gaga after the inauguration.

CHAPTER 8

SUPER BOWL POET

The **inauguration** had made Gorman a star. And it wasn't long before she was back in the national spotlight. In late January, the National Football League made an exciting announcement. Gorman would be performing a poem before the Super Bowl that February.

Gorman was the first poet to perform at a Super Bowl. Several days before the event, Gorman recorded her performance of her poem on video. On the day of the Super Bowl, the video was broadcast into millions of homes across the nation.

Later that month, Gorman appeared on the cover of *Time* magazine. The issue featured a conversation between Gorman and former First Lady Michelle Obama. In it, Gorman discussed how she was handling her sudden rise to fame. She said it was important to think about the bigger picture. She said, "You really have to crown yourself with the belief that what I'm about and what I'm here for is way beyond this moment."

AMANDA GORMAN
INAUGURAL US YOUTH POET LAUREATE

Gorman's Super Bowl poem was called "Chorus of the Captains." It honored three people who had done important work during the COVID-19 pandemic.

CHAPTER 9

THE FUTURE IS GORMAN

Gorman was still amazed by her sudden fame. She felt like she was dreaming. After an exciting start to 2021, she got back to her life in Los Angeles. She continued to promote **literacy**, education, and poetry.

In September, Gorman's two books came out. One was a poetry collection titled *The Hill We Climb*. It included her **inauguration** poem. The other was a picture book called *Change Sings: A Children's **Anthem***. The book featured **rhyming** text that encouraged readers to make a difference in the world.

Many new fans of Gorman wondered what was next for the star poet. Gorman didn't want to compete with what she'd already done. She just wanted to continue on the path she was on. "For me," she said, "that just means using my poetry to touch and heal and impact as many people as possible."

Gorman talks about running for president in 2036. "It's not that I want to run," she says. "It's that I'm going to run."

TIMELINE

1998
Amanda S.C. Gorman is born on March 7 in Los Angeles, California.

2015
Amanda publishes a book of her poems called *The One for Whom Food Is Not Enough*.

2017
Gorman is named the first National Youth Poet Laureate.

2014
Amanda is named the first Youth Poet Laureate of Los Angeles.

2016
Gorman founds One Pen One Page. She begins studying at Harvard University.

2020

Gorman graduates from Harvard and moves back to Los Angeles.

February 2021

Gorman performs a poem that is broadcast before the Super Bowl.

January 2021

Gorman recites a poem at the inauguration of President Joe Biden. She becomes the youngest inaugural poet in US history.

September 2021

Gorman publishes a poetry collection and a children's picture book.

GLOSSARY

anthem—a song of gladness or patriotism.

auditory—of or relating to hearing.

COVID-19—a serious illness that first appeared in late 2019.

disorder—a physical or mental condition that is not normal or healthy.

document—to create a record of something through writing, video, or pictures.

empathy—the understanding and sharing of another person's feelings.

empowering—to promote or influence someone becoming stronger and more confident, especially in taking control of their life and claiming their rights.

impediment—a condition that makes it difficult to speak normally.

inaugurate (ih-NAW-gyuh-rayt)—to swear into a political office. The ceremony in which a person is inaugurated is an inauguration. Something related to an inauguration is inaugural.

literacy—the state of being able to read and write.

mantra—a word or phrase that is repeated often or that expresses someone's basic beliefs.

pandemic—an outbreak of a disease that spreads quickly throughout the world.

podium—a raised platform that a speaker or performer stands on.

poet laureate—a poet who is honored by being chosen for an official position by a ruler or government.

rhyming—having words or lines ending with similar sounds.

sociology—the science of how people relate to one another and to their surroundings.

unrest—a situation in which many of the people in a country are angry and hold protests or act violently.

virtual reality—surroundings created by a computer that a person can affect and interact with.

ONLINE RESOURCES

Booklinks
NONFICTION NETWORK
FREE! ONLINE NONFICTION RESOURCES

To learn more about Amanda Gorman, please visit **abdobooklinks.com** or scan this QR code. These links are routinely monitored and updated to provide the most current information available.

INDEX